ENDS OF THE EARTH

THE WORLD'S REMOTE AND WILD PLACES

Antarctica

Kellie McDonald

7466345

© 1997 Ogma Writers
Published by Heinemann Library
an imprint of Reed Educational & Professional Publishing
500 Coventry Lane
Crystal Lake, IL 60014

All rights reserved. No part of this publication may be reproduced, stored in a retrieval system, or transmitted in any form by any means (electronic, mechanical, photocopying, recording or otherwise) without the prior written permission of the publisher.

Library of Congress Cataloging-in-Publication Data

McDonald, Kellie, 1970-
Antarctica / Kellie McDonald.
p. cm. -- (Ends of the earth)
Includes index.
Summary: Describes the geography, wildlife, and exploration of the world's fifth largest continent, Antarctica.
ISBN 0-431-06934. 4 (lib. bdg.)
1. Antarctica--Juvenile literature. [1. Antarctica.] I Title.
II. Series.
G863.M42 1997
919.8'904--dc21

97-1929
CIP
AC

01 00 99 98 97
10 9 8 7 6 5 4 3 2 1

Designed by David Doyle and Irwin Liaw
Edited by Stephen Dobney
Front and back cover photographs courtesy of Peter C. Gill
Picture research by Ogma Writers
Illustrations by Andrew Plant
Production by Elena Cementon
Printed in Hong Kong by H&Y Printing Limited

Every attempt has been made to trace and acknowledge copyright. Where the attempt has been unsuccessful, the publisher would be pleased to hear from the copyright owner so any omission or error can be rectified.

Contents

Part 1 A Frozen Continent

Antarctica: the last wilderness 4
The buried land 6
The Southern Ocean 8
The big chill 10
A scientific storehouse 12
Confronting the unexpected 14

Part 2 Antarctic Wildlife

Plants in a desert of snow 16
Small links in the chain 18
Whales 20
Penguins 22
The remarkable emperor 24
Seals 26
Fish 28
Seabirds 30

Part 3 Exploring the Land of the South Pole

Early sightings 32
Feet on icy land 34
Heroic explorers 36
Mawson: a case study in survival 38

Part 4 Modern Issues in an Old World

Technology on ice 40
The ozone "hole" 42
Environmental concerns 44
Toward a world park 46

Glossary 47
Index 48

Antarctica: the last wilderness

Doomed by nature?

In 1773, after circumnavigating Antarctica, Captain James Cook proclaimed:

> *I can be so bold to say no man will venture farther south than I have done and that the lands to the south will never be explored ... doomed by nature never once to feel the warmth of sun's rays, but to be buried in everlasting snow and ice.*

Fortunately, Cook's predictions turned out to be wrong.

Antarctica, the world's fifth largest continent, deserves the attention of all nations sharing planet Earth. From scientists' observations of this uniquely preserved area, we are learning that this remote region plays a vital, though quiet, role in the fragile balance of the Earth's ecosystems. Information collected from the Antarctic wilderness tells us not only about bacteria, penguins, glaciers, and seals, but also about the rest of the world and beyond. For example, scientists at NASA study Antarctica's Dry Valleys to learn about Mars, while meteorologists study Antarctica's weather patterns to learn about world weather, both past and present.

Figure 1 The vast continent and its wildlife are studied by scientists from all over the world. The Adelie penguins shown here are just one of the many species that are monitored.

(Photo courtesy of Peter C. Gill)

In the beginning

Antarctica has not always been a continent of ice and snow. Scientists believe that 560 million years ago it was part of a supercontinent called Gondwana, a land mass including Australia, Africa, South America, India, and New Zealand. The discovery in Antarctica of a seed fern also found in India, South America, and Africa adds weight to this theory. Evidence suggests that as late as 70 million years ago Gondwana's climate was semi-tropical, supporting dense forests and unknown animals and marine life, including giant reptiles and small bony fish.

Fossil remains uncovered in Antarctica suggest that dinosaurs also existed in the region. *Leaellynasura amicagraphica* was a dinosaur whose large optic lobes may have helped it to see better in the low light of winter. It is thought this creature lived in the area between Australia and Antarctica.

Scientists believe that the supercontinent broke apart over millions of years. The final separation of Antarctica from Australia is estimated to have happened 56 million years ago.

Figure 3 Gondwana, the supercontinent that included present-day South America, Australasia, Africa, India, and Antarctica, began to separate about 160 million years ago. During the Jurassic period (about 200 million years ago), the land mass was covered in thick forests, providing a home for dinosaurs and other animals.

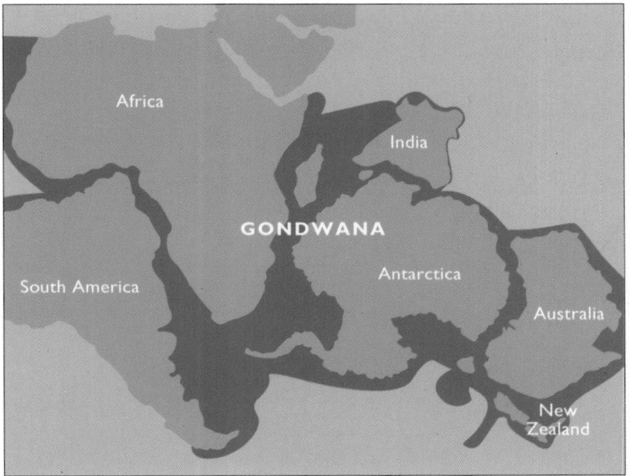

Antarctica is the coldest place on Earth, with the lowest temperature ever recorded: –129.3°F (–89.6°C); cold so severe it freezes skin in 60 seconds. It is also the driest, windiest, and highest region on Earth.

Figure 2 (below) Although areas of rock can be seen at this site near Cape Hallet, less than 1 percent of Antarctica is actually free of ice. The remaining 99.6 percent of the continent holds around 90 percent of all the ice on Earth.

(Photo courtesy of Peter C. Gill)

The buried land

Today, Antarctica is separated from other continents by the stormy Southern Ocean, although technically its boundary is defined by the Antarctic Convergence. The Convergence, or Polar Front, is a 25-mile-wide band of water where cold currents sink below the warmer waters, creating a natural division in the marine environment. The Convergence marks the entry into the vast region of the Antarctic wilderness.

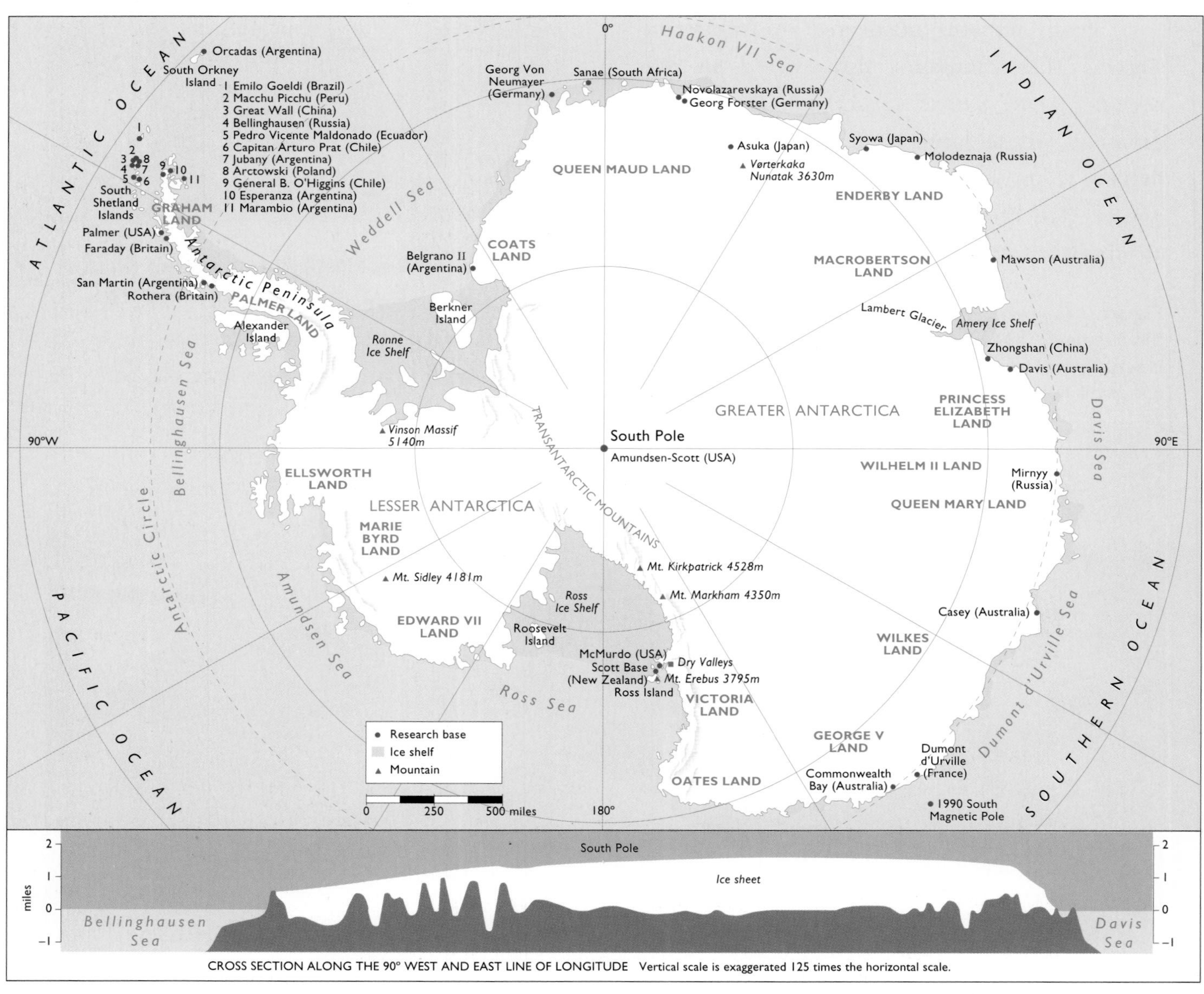

CROSS SECTION ALONG THE 90° WEST AND EAST LINE OF LONGITUDE Vertical scale is exaggerated 125 times the horizontal scale.

Figure 5 (left) The Canada Glacier; glaciers such as this one drain the Antarctic icecap. The largest glacier, known as the Lambert Glacier, is almost 248 miles long and 25 miles wide.

Figure 6 (right) Geologists have discovered that rock formations at Mt. Wellington in Tasmania (shown here) are similar to those found in the Trans-Antarctic Mountains. The rocks, known as Ferrar dolerite, are a type of basalt.

(Photo courtesy of Department of Tourism, Sport and Recreation, Tasmania)

The Antarctic continent makes up 10 percent of the Earth's land mass, but in form and shape it is unlike any other continent. It is divided into Greater and Lesser Antarctica by the Trans-Antarctic Mountains, a range 2980 miles long. East of the range, Greater Antarctica rises in a towering ice dome, 13,940 feet above sea level at its highest point. In the west lies Lesser Antarctica, older and half as large as the eastern region. Geologists believe that Lesser Antarctica is actually three large masses of rock welded together by the cover of the icecap.

Figure 4 (facing page) This map of Antarctica shows the location of the permanent research bases. The cross section shows the incredible thickness of the ice sheet.

Highs and lows

This icecap locks up 70 percent of the world's fresh water, making Antarctica both the lowest and the highest continent on Earth. Its height averages 7500 feet, the greatest average height above sea level of any continent. However, the ice is so heavy that it pushes most of the rocky land down below sea level, in some places to a depth of 1.5 miles.

The huge Antarctic ice sheet moves slowly but constantly outward from the center of the continent toward the coast in the form of glaciers. Although glaciers are often described as rivers of ice, they do not flow like water; instead they slide or creep along, pulled downward by gravity.

Usually there is a thin layer of water between the ice and the rock underneath; if there is no water, the glacier sticks, frozen to its base. When this occurs, the molecules of the ice crystals rearrange so that they glide over one another.

The Southern Ocean

The Roaring Forties

All sailors know that the Southern Ocean is one of the most treacherous bodies of water on the globe. Known for its violent changes, extreme winds, and monstrous waves, the Southern Ocean extends over 14 million square miles south of the Antarctic Convergence. Winds blowing from the icecap can reach speeds of 186 miles per hour over the water, while strong westerly winds create currents four times stronger than the Gulf Stream. The seas covering the mid-latitudes (40, 50, and 60 degrees south) are particularly infamous, nicknamed by sailors the Roaring Forties, the Furious Fifties, and the Screaming Sixties.

The dramatic difference in temperature between the Antarctic and the surrounding warmer ocean creates low-pressure systems that become cyclones. Forming between 60 and 65 degrees south, these cyclones circulate winds in a clockwise direction, and so move warmer air from their northern sector to the south, and cooler air from their southern sector northward. In this way heat and humidity are moved from subtropical regions toward the polar region. Because the systems are intense, the winds are very strong. The cyclones move slowly toward the Antarctic coast, where they die out.

Ice and icebergs

Another hazard facing ships attempting to cross the Southern Ocean is the ice. During the polar winter, as much as 8 million square miles or 56 percent of the ocean's surface freezes. This is not just a problem for ships: Antarctic wildlife that feed from the ocean are forced to travel farther north to reach their food supply as a huge expanse of water turns into unbroken ice.

Figure 7 Most Southern Ocean icebergs originally break off from ice shelves such as this. Ice shelves make up about 30 per cent of the Antarctic coastline.

(Photo courtesy of Peter C. Gill)

It is estimated that the volume of the icebergs that break off the Antarctic continent each year is equal to half of the water used in the world annually. Most icebergs break away from the ice shelves, which are huge floating blocks

Figure 8 Huge drifting icebergs are a hazard for ships navigating the Southern Ocean.

(Photo courtesy of Peter C. Gill)

On November 12, 1956 the USS *Glacier* spotted an iceberg as large as Belgium. The massive block of floating ice was 208 miles long and 60 miles wide.

Traveling to Antarctica

Although it is possible to fly to the Antarctic, many people still travel by ship. The most popular point of departure is Port Stanley in the Falkland Islands. Crossing from this point to the Antarctic Peninsula can take several weeks in bad weather, or only three days in good conditions, traveling at an average speed of 10 knots. Even with today's technology, however, many sailors are still wary of sailing across the stormy Southern Ocean.

of ice anchored to the land at several points below sea level. Some of these ice shelves, like the Ross Ice Shelf, form in slabs as large as France. Other icebergs come from glaciers or ice cliffs, but these are usually smaller in size. The process of icebergs breaking away from shelves or glaciers is often referred to as "calving."

Once they have broken away, the icebergs are carried northwest by a strong ocean current known as the circumpolar current. The average speed of an iceberg is estimated to be 8 miles per day. Those reaching the Antarctic Convergence change their direction and begin to drift to the northeast.

(Photo courtesy of Louise Crossley)

Figure 9 (above)
Ships crossing the Southern Ocean often have to cope with rough, unpredictable seas and gale-force winds.

Although it may take many years before an iceberg melts, cracks inside the ice often break the huge chunks into smaller fragments before the melt occurs.

The big chill

How cold is cold?

In every region of Antarctica the temperatures are cold: the low-lying coastal areas average around –10°F; up on the icecap at 3200 feet, the average is –4°F; and at the highest points around 12,000 feet above sea level it is –76°F.

In midsummer, the Antarctic is exposed to a greater amount of radiation than the Equator receives at any period of the year, but the southern continent only absorbs a very small amount. One reason for this is the angle of exposure: the sun does not climb very high above the horizon, and its rays are spread out over a wide area. In the tropics the sun rises high in the sky, and its rays are concentrated in a small area.

Another factor adding to the cold is the mirror effect produced by the ice, which covers 99.6 percent of Antarctica. As the ice is white, it reflects the sun's rays. On average, 80 percent of short-wave radiation is reflected back into the atmosphere, compared with only 15 to 35 percent in areas that are free of ice and snow.

Just as extreme as the temperatures are the winds that rage across the Antarctic continent. Because Antarctica is dome-shaped, the cold air in the center flows down and outward, gathering speed as it travels toward the coast. These down-flowing (katabatic) winds are pushed along by the force of gravity and reach speeds of more than 50 miles per hour. As they reach the coast, the katabatic winds collide with warmer air coming in from the ocean. This creates a narrow storm region of severe blizzards, cloud, and fog.

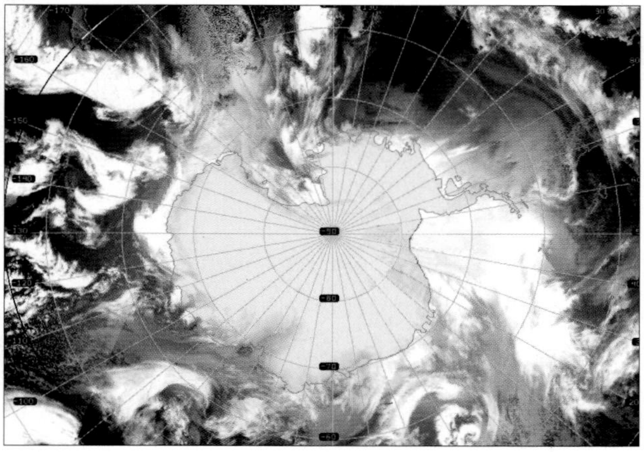

(Photo courtesy of AMRC/SSEC/UW-Madison on McIDAS)

Figure 10 Produced from data from several different U.S. satellites, this image clearly shows the powerful winds circling Antarctica.

An icy desert

Antarctica is the Earth's largest desert. Snowfall on the highest plateau in Antarctica is equal to the rainfall received in the Sahara Desert in north Africa. The snow that does fall may come from one of the many blizzards that rage across the Antarctic. Although it is often slightly warmer during a blizzard, the wind speed increases to an average of 93 miles per hour. In this kind of weather you may only be able to see up to 3 feet around you. Such raging blizzards can last for several days, making it difficult to do anything outside.

(Photo courtesy of Australian Bureau of Meteorology)

Figure 11 (left) Studying Antarctic weather patterns can be difficult for meteorologists because of the extreme cold. To help collect information, automatic weather stations, floating buoys, and satellites are also used.

(Photo courtesy of Australian Bureau of Meteorology)

Figure 12 Weather balloons are used to help gather data about Antarctic weather, and about the changing levels of gases in the atmosphere.

We are accustomed to days that are roughly 12 hours of light and 12 hours of dark, so it is difficult to imagine the Antarctic's days, which can be continuously light or continuously dark, depending on the season. From 66 degrees south—a line called the Antarctic Circle—to the South Pole, the sun does not rise at all during the middle of winter. At the South Pole, the sun sets only once—for half the year. This means for half the year it is always light at the Pole, and for the other half of the year it is always dark.

A scientific storehouse

Antarctica not only provides us with a wealth of information about the South Polar region, it also contains clues about the history of the planet, and even the universe.

Recorded history

Trapped in the multiple layers of ice covering the continent of Antarctica is a record of the climatic changes that have taken place on the Earth. To investigate, scientists drill down into the ice and pull out long solid tubes known as ice cores. Usually, the ice cores are removed in 3 foot lengths by mechanical drills. Holes have been drilled as deep as 1.25 miles, one reaching the bedrock. Drilling these kinds of holes may take up to 10 years. During this time the ice sheet is moving, causing the ice core hole to curve.

The scientists take all kinds of measurements from the cores, such as the different amounts of oxygen and hydrogen. The proportions of oxygen and hydrogen vary between summer and winter, so scientists can date the snow by counting the number of winters. This is a similar method to dating trees by counting their rings.

The ice cores contain a lot of other valuable information. Scientists have learned that during a period of time about 18,000 years ago, dust levels were higher than they are now. This suggests that there were bigger deserts on Earth, and stronger winds capable of carrying the dust long distances. Scientists can also tell when volcanic eruptions have occurred in the last 4000 years, and can measure air bubbles trapped in the ice to find out the levels of greenhouse gases such as carbon dioxide (CO_2).

(Photo courtesy of Louise Crossley)

Meteorites

Since 1974, more than 14,000 meteorites have been discovered in the Antarctic region, including a rare nickel-iron meteorite containing minute diamond fragments that would have formed when the meteorite crashed

Figure 14 a & b (right & far right) The conditions in the Dry Valleys are so similar to the surface of Mars (shown here) that NASA tested some of its equipment in the valleys before launching its *Viking* probe to Mars.

(Photos courtesy of NASA/Melbourne Planetarium)

Figure 13 (above) The Dry Valleys are areas of Antarctica that are mostly free of ice. Such areas are known as oases. Although some snow can be seen in this picture, other oases have had no snow, rain, or ice fall in at least two million years.

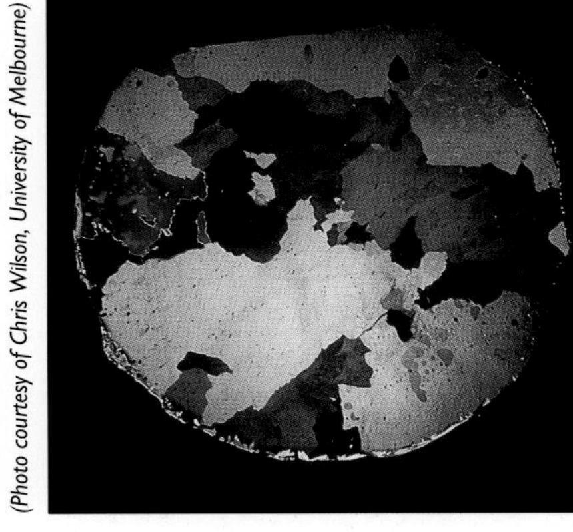

(Photo courtesy of Chris Wilson, University of Melbourne)

Figure 15 (left) Seen under a special light, this 0.028 inch thick section of ice is from a core drilled at Law Dome. By comparing it with other sections from the same core, scientists can estimate the age of the ice. The contents of the ice sample can also provide valuable information about the history of the Earth's weather and environment.

into the Earth. Usually, falling meteorites are lost at sea, or land in remote regions where they are worn away by the weather. In the Antarctic, they are trapped in the ice which then moves them slowly toward the sea. Some become caught behind mountain ranges and, as the dry winds wear away the layers of ice, the meteorites come closer to the surface.

Australian explorer Sir Douglas Mawson discovered the first Antarctic meteorite in 1912. After 50 years without further finds, another three were discovered by U.S. and Soviet scientists. Recent discoveries have included a lunar fragment believed to have been chipped off the moon by a large asteroid. Another two fragments, thought to originate from Mars, have also been uncovered, although scientists are not sure how the rocks reached the Earth without vaporizing.

Confronting the unexpected

Dog suns and halos

Despite being covered in ice and snow, the Antarctic is not a bland desert of endless white. Ice crystals suspended in the air and clouds reflect and refract the light of the sun and moon, creating dazzling displays in a dramatic range of shapes and colors. Around the sun and moon, halos form in the shape of circles, spots, or arcs commonly known as "dog" or "mock" suns and moons. Sun pillars—vertical pillars of light—also appear, shooting up from the horizon, while icebows (like rainbows) lay their colorful displays on the ground.

Aurora australis

Called "the great burning of the sky" by the Maori people of New Zealand, aurora australis (the southern lights) is a spectacular display of red, violet, and green curtains of light that hover, ghost-like, over the night sky. This kind of display occurs at both the North and South Poles when particles with very strong magnetic properties meet particles entering the Earth's atmosphere from the sun and create storm-like magnetic activity. The colors in the aurora depend on the type and amount of gases colliding in the atmosphere: nitrogen creates violet, while atomic oxygen creates red and green. The activity producing the aurora also creates heat. This makes the upper atmosphere expand and can interfere with radio and satellite communication.

Whiteout

A more dangerous Antarctic illusion is whiteout. Whiteout occurs when the cloudy sky and the snow-covered land are evenly colored so there are no shadows. Although the air itself may be clear, the dips, crevices, and upward slopes are not recognized by a person's brain. Travelers may walk up and down a hill thinking they have walked a flat surface. Whiteout also makes it difficult to judge how close or how far away an object may be. This can also confuse birds and they may crash while trying to land because they are unable to judge the surface of the snow.

Figure 16 The combination of ice crystal clouds and sunlight can create spectacular displays, including halos which arc or circle around the sun or moon.

(Photo courtesy of C. Blobel, Australian Bureau of Meteorology)

(Photo courtesy of Greg Mortimer)

Figure 17 (left)
A sun pillar appears in the Antarctic sky as a vertical line reaching down to the horizon. If you look closely at this picture you can see the straight yellow line of a pillar.

The leader of the Australian Mawson station in 1991, Louise Crossley, described a scene during an Antarctic winter: "The low sun creates brilliant orange and red sunsets in the northwest, grading to the palest pink and mauve to the south where the icecap glows a pure translucent blue. Dark purple mountains pierce the surface, and over all, a full moon is rising."

(Photo courtesy of A. Nutley, Australian Antarctic Division)

Figure 18 (above) Aurora australis, also known as the Southern Lights, is caused when solar winds containing magnetic particles from the sun collide with the Earth's magnetic field.

Plants in a desert of snow

With most of the land mass buried under the ice, only 2 percent of the Antarctic can support plant life. The few places in which plants can grow are the Dry Valleys, bare rocky areas, and stretches where melting snow in the summer nourishes growth. Even in these places, few species can endure the low temperatures, strong winds, and unpredictable water supply. As a result, there is little plant growth on the continent. There are no flowers or trees: flora is limited to lichens, mosses, algae, and fungi.

Ancient plants

The toughest Antarctic plant is lichen—some have been known to live for more than 2000 years. One of the main reasons lichens survive the cold is that the acids and proteins that make up a large part of the plant do not freeze until the temperature drops below –4°F. Several kinds of lichens also freeze-dry in the winter and then revive when there is enough liquid or water vapor available.

Lichens are actually part algae, part fungus. Most of the 350 known species grow on stones and rocks and many have a tough, dark-colored outer layer that holds in moisture and warmth. About 125 species have been found in the center of the continent, and 150 on the peninsula and islands. Growth is slow—lichens expand only 0.6 inches every 100 years.

Lichen also provides a base for moss. There are 85 species of moss on the main continent, peninsula, and islands. Moss also grows very slowly, and mainly during the summer months when there is a little more warmth.

Figure 19 (above) Although there are no trees on the Antarctic continent, lichen (shown here) and moss provide occasional patches of orange, brown, and green.

Only two species of flowering plant have been found in Antarctica—hair grass and pearlwort—both of which only grow on the northern peninsula. Fungi, bacteria, and algae have also been found in cracks and air pockets in light-colored rocks (through which sunlight can enter). The surface of the rock protects the plants

(Photo courtesy of Simon Ward)

Figure 20 (above) Antarctic moss grows at an average rate of 0.6 inches every 100 years. Damage to moss or lichen takes years to repair.

Figure 21 In Antarctica most lichens grow on rocks and stones. Despite the extreme cold, some lichen have been known to survive for more than 2000 years.

(Photo courtesy of Simon Ward)

Colored snow

Although there are no stretches of grass, large tracts of snow are periodically covered in splashes of green, yellow or, more commonly, red. Mainly occurring near the coast, particularly on the Antarctic Peninsula, this "bleeding" is caused by single-celled algae. As the algae absorb the sun's light in a process known as photosynthesis, their pigments (colors in the plants' tissues) are released and stain the melting snow. There are approximately 300 types of non-marine algae growing in the Antarctic.

from the dry wind, but also allows carbon dioxide, minerals, and tiny amounts of moisture to filter in, providing the plants with food and water. Some of these species are believed to have lived inside their ancient rock homes for more than 200,000 years.

Under the water

The seabed beneath the ice is where most Antarctic plants grow. Silt, sand, and small bolders from melting icebergs add minerals to the water. These, combined with high oxygen levels created by stormy seas and long summer daylight, produce a rich "soil." As a result, seaweed and algae flourish on parts of the sea floor, as do animals such as corals, sea cucumbers, and sponges.

Small links in the chain

The food chain supporting Antarctic wildlife is an unusual one. Two well-recognized members in the chain are phytoplankton (a tiny plant) and krill (a small, shrimp-like crustacean).

Phytoplankton

Phytoplankton usually grow on the water's surface where they can use the sunlight to produce energy. During the Antarctic summer, when there are several months of continual daylight, these tiny plants thrive. The Southern Ocean supplies the phytoplankton with large amounts of nitrates and phosphates, but the churning currents also spread the plants unpredictably across the sea.

Krill

Phytoplankton is essential in the diet of Antarctic krill. These tiny crustaceans are the staple food for many species of seals, squid, fish, whales, and Antarctic birds. Krill have a very high protein content (as much as 50 percent after processing), as well as vitamins A and D, various B-group vitamins, and minerals such as calcium, magnesium, copper, iron, and phosphorous. Some scientists believe that krill could become a source of protein for developing nations. However, concerns have been voiced about harvesting krill because they support so much of the continent's wildlife.

Japan, Poland, and countries of the former U.S.S.R. are the main krill fishers, although the catch has decreased from a peak of 581,000 tons harvested in 1981–82. Krill have been marketed in cheese spreads and soups, and as krill sticks, but the majority of the catch is currently used for livestock feed.

Until recently, scientists thought that krill lived for only two to three years, and reproduced rapidly. However, scientists have now discovered that krill can live for up to eleven years, and can shrink themselves to survive food shortages, making their age more difficult to estimate. These new facts have made some people question how quickly krill populations can recover from being harvested. Without full knowledge of how fishing might threaten the population, caution must be taken to protect krill and all the life-forms they support.

One problem with krill fishing is that, as the krill begin to decompose, their fluoride levels increase to as much as 24 times the amount allowed by U.S. food regulations.

To stop this occurring, krill must be frozen quickly once caught and stored at temperatures below –4°F. Advances in refrigeration make such snap freezing possible.

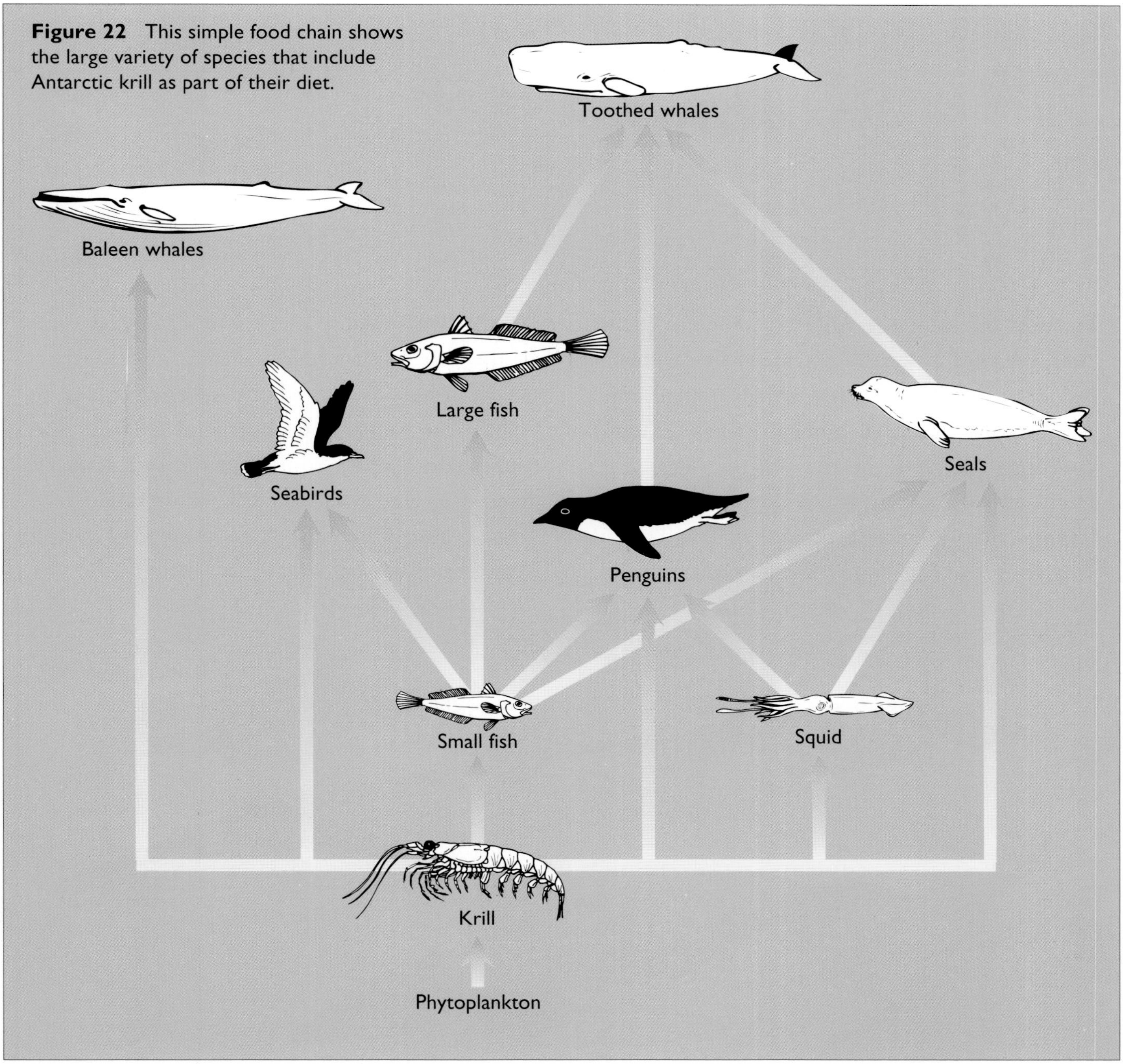

Figure 22 This simple food chain shows the large variety of species that include Antarctic krill as part of their diet.

Toothed whales

Baleen whales

Large fish

Seabirds

Seals

Penguins

Small fish

Squid

Krill

Phytoplankton

"Krill" means "small-fry." The name was used by Norwegian whalers to describe these crustaceans, which are only 2 inches long.

Although small, their total population in Antarctic waters is estimated to be more than 600 billion.

Figure 23 In some countries krill are a source of food for humans and livestock, and are also fed to fish on fish farms.

(Photo courtesy of S. Nicol)

Whales

For over 60 years, the Antarctic whale population was paid unwanted attention by commercial whalers who saw these remarkable mammals as potential money-makers. Due to the huge "success" of the whaling industry, many species are now endangered. Whales found in the Antarctic region include baleen whales: blue, fin, right, sei, humpback, and minke, and odontoceti (toothed) whales: orca (killer whales) and sperm whales.

Seven of the eleven species of baleen whales migrate from northern tropical and subtropical waters to feed in the rich summer waters of the Antarctic. The adult blue whale eats as much as 3 to 4 tons every day during the feeding season.

Figure 24 Antarctic whales.

(Photo courtesy of Greg Mortimer)

Figure 25 (below) A Southern Ocean whale blows out air and water in a steam-like spray.

(Photo courtesy of Greg Mortimer)

Figure 26 (above) Although this killer whale looks harmless floating amongst the ice, it is actually a fierce pack hunter. The tongue of the baleen whale is just one of its favorite foods.

The largest of the odontoceti whales, the male sperm whale, enters the Southern Ocean in search of squid. Up to 59 feet long and weighing as much as 75 tons, the males can dive to depths of more than 3000 feet, and can hold their breath for between 60 and 90 minutes. The odontoceti whales not only have teeth, they also have two nasal passages (but only one nostril).

At the top of the sperm whale's head is a cavity filled with clear wax called spermaceti oil, which the whale uses to control its buoyancy. By diverting its blood flow, the whale can heat or cool the oil, changing it from liquid to solid. This helps the whale when diving and returning to the surface. Unfortunately, whalers also considered this oil valuable for making detergent and lubricants.

The southern bottlenose whale also has oil, contained in a large melon-like lump on its head. The bottlenose is sighted far less often than the sperm whale. It can stay under water for up to one hour.

Baleen whales have giant sieves on the sides of their mouths instead of teeth. They all use their bristle-fringed baleen plates to strain the krill, but different whales use different methods. In swallow feeding, the whale gulps a mouthful of ocean, squeezing out the water by tightening its throat and pushing its tongue to the roof of its mouth. Blue, fin, and minke whales feed in this way. Sei and right whales swim though a krill swarm, head half out, mouth slightly open, skimming their food out of the water.

Humpbacks swim under water, blowing a net of bubbles that trap the krill ready for eating.

Killer, or orca, whales are also found in the Southern Ocean. These whales prey on other whales and seals, hunting in groups or packs known as pods. The fastest of the whales, the killers are known to break through thin ice, forcing seals to scramble to thicker areas. Not to be outwitted, the whales sometimes leap into the air, bombing the water so the resulting wave washes the seals from their ice-raft.

Penguins

Seven of the world's eighteen species of penguins can be found in Antarctica (see box), and the continent hosts an estimated population of 17 to 20 million breeding pairs. Although they are unable to fly and are very awkward on land, these birds are excellent swimmers. They use their webbed feet, rudder-like tail, and powerful flippers to move themselves easily through the water.

Penguins are well prepared to survive the freezing conditions of the continent. Covered in overlapping, waterproof feathers that trap air close to their skin, the birds are further insulated with an underlayer of down. They also carry a large amount of fat which both warms and nourishes them. In spite of the cold—both in the ocean and on land—the penguins can sometimes overheat. To ventilate, or cool themselves, they ruffle their feathers, or allow heat to escape through featherless patches on their feet, flippers, and faces.

Figure 27 Very young Adelie chicks are too small to keep themselves warm and must huddle close to one of their parents. After about two weeks they have usually gained enough weight to wander away briefly on their own.

(Photo courtesy of Peter C. Gill)

The penguin's coat is vital for winter survival, so before the dark season arrives, penguins shed their feathers and replace them with a whole new set. Because molting uses a lot of energy, the penguins first build up the weight they lost during chick rearing. Over a period of almost three weeks there is silence in the chinstrap penguin colonies as each bird sheds 3 to 4 pounds of feathers—about one-third of its body weight.

An unusual characteristic of Antarctic penguins concerns their underwater vision. Standing on land the penguin's sight is blurred, but with eyes that are particularly sensitive to blue, green, and violet light, its vision in the ocean is sharp and clear.

Underwater living also requires other adaptations: because of the high salt content in the seawater, penguins are equipped with an unusual method for removing excess salt from their bodies. Special glands extract the salt from the penguin's bloodstream, filtering it out through the bird's nose.

Penguins have a clever social arrangement to help protect their chicks from natural predators. While the parents search for food, the

(Photo courtesy of Peter C. Gill)

Figure 28 (right) Rockhopper penguins (shown here) and macaroni penguins belong to a group known as crested penguins. Both species are known for their aggressive behavior. The sub-Antarctic islands, which are not as cold as the Antarctic continent, provide excellent breeding grounds for the penguins.

(Photo courtesy of *Museum of Victoria, Australia*)

Figure 29 (left) Because king penguins must feed their chicks during the winter, they need access to the sea. As a result, they breed on the sub-Antarctic islands where the ice cover is not as great.

young gather together in nurseries, huddling to protect themselves from storms or dangerous animals. When parents return with food they find their own young by calling them. To make sure they don't feed another chick in the huddle, the parent calls, then runs away from the nursery. The hungry young chick leaves the group, eager to catch its parent and its dinner.

The penguins' enemies include the skua, leopard seal, killer whale, and sea lion. Human interference that alters, pollutes, or disturbs their environment is also a threat.

THE SEVEN ANTARCTIC PENGUIN SPECIES

Adelie
Average 11 lb; 28 inches
- most numerous of the seven species
- thought to navigate by the sun

Chinstrap
Average 10 lb; 27 inches
- nests on rocky slopes
- named for a line of black feathers on their white chin

Emperor
Average 65 lb; 46 inches
- heaviest and largest Antarctic penguin
- only penguin that breeds in winter

Gentoo
Average 12 lb; 28 inches
- fastest swimmer (up to 17 mph)
- builds a nest from seaweed and small rocks

King
Average 33 lb; 38 inches
- breeds two chicks every three years
- record dive of 884 feet

Macaroni
Average 9 lb; 28 inches
- named after extravagantly dressed eighteenth century British travelers
- lays two eggs: one half size (usually only one survives)

Rockhopper
Average 5.5 lb; 22 inches
- smallest Antarctic penguin
- most aggressive of the penguin family

The remarkable emperor

When the thick crust of winter sea ice starts forming around the continent, most animals escape to the north where temperatures are slightly warmer. Emperor penguins are the exception. Beginning their breeding when the others have finished, they are the only species to incubate their eggs on ice in the bitterly cold Antarctic winter.

The cycle begins in March and April on an open area of flat ice where a large number of penguins gather to court. Courting is a loud affair because all the birds sing, establishing calls their mates will recognize among the crowd.

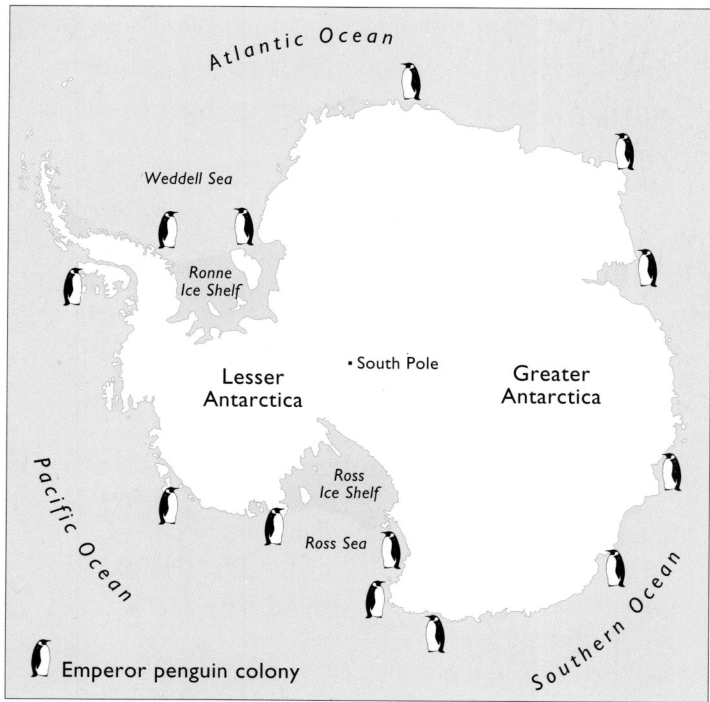

Figure 30 The location of emperor penguin colonies.

About six weeks later, the female lays her egg. Within a few hours she has passed it to the male who keeps it off the ice by balancing it on his feet. If the egg is to mature, it must be kept warm, so the male tucks it against a bare patch of skin near his stomach, and a special loose pocket of skin rolls over the egg, completely protecting it from the freezing air. The pouch is so effective that during the middle of winter it may be 140 degrees warmer than the outside temperature.

Once the egg has been transferred to the male, the female leaves for the ocean where she stays swimming and feeding for the next 65 days. The male is left alone with the vital task of incubating the egg. To survive in temperatures as low as –76°F, the emperor penguins huddle together, rotating the group so each takes a turn in the warmth at the center. The emperors are also equipped with special nasal passages that recycle 80 percent of the warmth usually lost in breathing.

The female penguin's return is timed for the hatching of the egg in July. Occasionally the chick arrives early and for 10 to 15 days the male is able to feed the young by regurgitating a milky liquid of protein and fat. Once the couple are reunited through their unique song, the female feeds the chick then moves it quickly onto her feet and covers it with a fold of skin.

It is then time for the male to feed: for 115 days from courtship to hatching of the

Winter breeding is undoubtedly a difficult undertaking, but the emperor penguins have little choice. They are the biggest of the Antarctic species and so need large amounts of food to survive. If the newly independent chicks were released to fend for themselves in autumn, they would be unlikely to survive because the food supply decreases before and during the winter. Late breeding means there is enough food for both young and old by summer.

Balloons carrying remote-controlled cameras are sometimes used to photograph penguin colonies from the air. Scientists use the photographs to estimate the number of penguins in each colony. In 1993 it was estimated that there were 195,000 breeding pairs of emperor penguins in Antarctica.

Under the Antarctic Treaty, an emperor penguin colony near Australia's Mawson research base has been declared a Special Protection Area, to minimize disruption to penguins during breeding.

(Photo courtesy of Peter C. Gill)

Figure 31 Only the emperor penguins breed on the fast ice during the winter months, rearing their chicks for independence by the time summer arrives.

chick, he has eaten no food. During this time, the male emperor loses 40 percent of his body weight; even when incubation has finished, his meal is still several days away across the ice.

Three weeks later, the male returns and the parents share the rearing of the chick. From six weeks old, the young penguin chicks can be gathered into nurseries while parents "go to work" to search for food.

Seals

With a scientific name meaning fin-footed (pinniped), it is clear that seals are designed for a life in the water. The Southern Ocean is not just any stretch of water, however. Each seal species in the Antarctic region is equipped with a special form of insulation, either fur or blubber, to survive the icy temperatures.

There are six species of seals living in Antarctica: crabeater, elephant, leopard, Ross, Weddell, and fur seals. Different seals are capable of living with different degrees of cold. In the south, Weddell seals can live in the fast ice while the Ross seals are located further north in the pack ice.

Measuring up to 16 feet and weighing up to 4 tonnes, the elephant seal was named for its size and because of the male's trunk-like "nose." This seal has been known to dive to depths of 4750 feet, and can remain under water for up to two hours.

The mating habits of elephant seals are unusual. Whereas other species mate in pairs or claim territory, the male elephant seal (the bull) collects females into harems. To claim a female, the bull often has to fight another hopeful male. Size usually determines fighting strength, and the more powerful bulls may have as many as 100 females grouped near them.

Determined to keep their harem, the bull may scare away rivals by making a loud roaring noise through its inflated trunk. If this fails, two bulls will fight, rearing up on their tails before thudding into each other with their head and body, and tearing at each other's necks with their teeth. As few as 30 percent of the bulls actually mate in a season; many return to the ocean with scars as their only trophy.

Another species noted for its violence is the leopard seal. Averaging 10 feet long, and weighing about 770 pounds, the leopard is a slim seal with a spotted stomach and a body designed for speed in hunting. Penguin chicks

Figure 33 Of all the mammals on Earth, the Weddell seal breeds furthest south, on the cold Antarctic fast ice that stays solid even during the summer months.

(Photo courtesy of Peter C. Gill)

(Photo courtesy of the Australian Department of Foreign Affairs & Trade)

Figure 32 This person has come too close to a group of elephant seals, and is being told to "back off." Fortunately, elephant seals do not eat people: their diet consists mainly of fish and squid.

entering the ocean for the first time are easy prey for the leopard seal. Leopards also eat adult penguins, occasionally crashing through the thinner ice to grab a meal. Crabeater seals are also part of their diet, as well as krill during the winter months.

With world numbers at 40 million, the **crabeater seal** is one of the most common larger mammals. The name of the species is definitely misleading since the main diet of the crabeater is not crab, but krill.

The smallest and rarest of the Antarctic seals is the **Ross seal** with an average length of 7.5 feet, a weight of 440 pounds, and an estimated population of 50,000 to 150,000. Because it is rare and difficult to sight, little is known about the habits of the Ross seal.

Spending most of the winter in the water, the **Weddell seal** uses its teeth to scrape ice clear from its underwater breathing hole. Unfortunately, this wears its teeth away and can cause gum abscesses that shorten its life span.

Of all the Antarctic varieties, the **fur seal** has been most sought after by humans because of the demand for its thick coat. The population of fur seals in Antarctica was severely threatened in the 1800s by sealers working the fur trade. In March 1978, hunting Antarctic fur seals was finally made illegal and the seals were listed as a protected species.

(Photo courtesy of the Australian Department of Foreign Affairs)

Figure 34 King penguins and seals on Macquarie Island. Although the king penguins have the land to themselves during winter, breeding season brings the seals.

Fish

While the Arctic is one of the world's major commercial fishing areas, the Antarctic has only 120 of the world's 20,000 recorded species of fish, mainly because it lacks suitable breeding areas. Spawning fish need shallows along the coast where their eggs can mature. With deep water even along the shoreline, the Antarctic continental shelf is unsuitable for this. Most of the fish living in the Antarctic are unique in some way, and are found only in the Southern Ocean.

Designed for survival

Antarctic fish are designed to survive in extreme conditions. One way they do this is to lay fewer, larger eggs. Whereas Arctic cod lay more than 6 million eggs, most Antarctic fish produce only a few thousand eggs. The smaller number of eggs allows the parents to give their young extra care until they can survive on their own.

Another remarkable feature is the low volume of red blood cells and hemoglobin found in most Antarctic fish. Hemoglobin is a red substance in the blood that carries oxygen through the body. One Antarctic species, the ice fish, has no hemoglobin at all, so its blood is almost clear. The ice fish survives in the Antarctic because it has a large volume of blood, a very big heart and blood vessels, and a heart rate almost ten times faster than similar fish that do have hemoglobin.

The freezing water temperatures also mean the ice fish needs less energy; in cold conditions most animals slow down, reducing the amount of oxygen they need to live on. In addition, the Southern Ocean contains very high levels of oxygen that can easily pass through the wide gills of ice fish. As an extra measure, ice fish also take in oxygen through their skin.

Sea water freezes at about 28.7°F. Antarctic fish, however, contain a type of "antifreeze" made of sugars and proteins that stops ice crystals from forming in severe cold. As a result, these fish can live successfully in waters as cold as 27°F.

Young fish grow very slowly in the extreme cold, and in the Antarctic both young and adult fish can be found in the same area. In spite of the small range of species, commercial fishing does occur in Antarctic waters. One problem associated with this fishing is that the fisheries do not regulate the size of their nets, so immature fish are often caught along with the adults, removing generations that have not yet bred. Restrictions may be necessary to make sure the fish populations are carefully maintained.

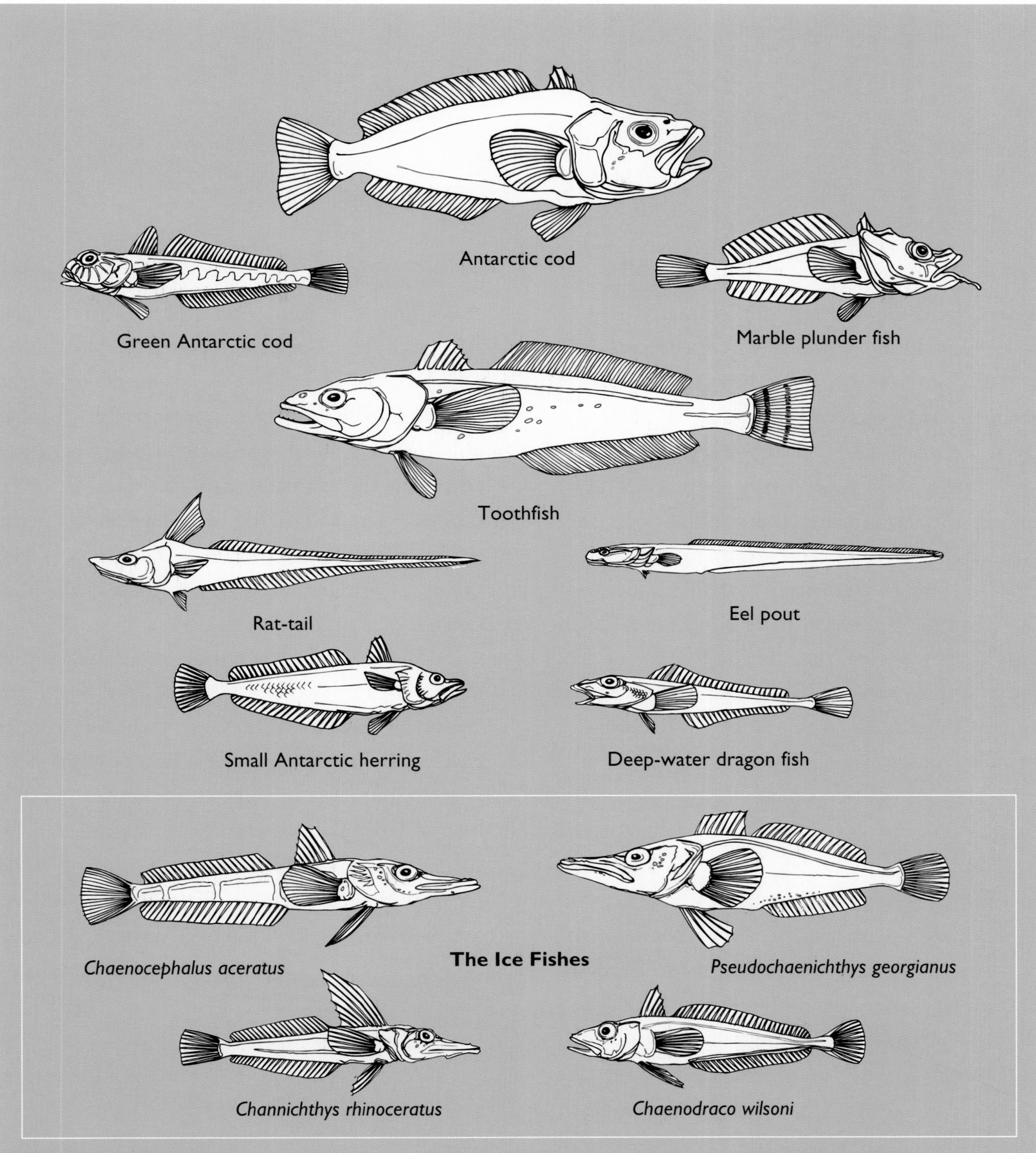

Figure 35 Antarctic fish

The Antarctic toothfish boasts some unusual features. Many fish similar to the toothfish live near the ocean floor as they do not have a gas-filled swim-bladder to make them float. The Antarctic toothfish, however, swims in middle-level waters because, unlike other fish, it has hollow vertebrae, large amounts of buoyant fat, and a skeleton made from cartilage, not bone, making it much lighter than the average fish.

Seabirds

Seventy million seabirds are estimated to live in the Antarctic. However, these represent only 50 of the 300 or more known species of seabirds. They include four species of albatross; twenty-three petrels, shearwaters, and prions; seven penguins; four storm petrels and two diving petrels; three terns; two skuas; one gull; two sheathbills; and one cormorant.

Although the ocean is their major feeding ground, the seabirds do need land. With only 2 percent of the continent free of ice, most species rely on the cliffs, coastal areas, and inland slopes of the Antarctic islands for breeding places.

The Antarctic climate creates other difficulties for the seabirds. With only a short summer in which to breed, many of the birds, including the albatross, lay only one egg. Though the incubation is shared between the partners, the process still takes up to 80 days. Difficulties arise once the chick hatches as there is often not enough food to feed both parents and their young. Usually half the chicks die, either from starvation or from attacks by land predators. Because the incubation period is long, adults and chicks are on the land for a considerable time, increasing the risk of such attacks.

There are four species of albatross in the Antarctic, the best known being the wandering albatross whose 12-foot wingspan makes it the largest seabird on Earth. This incredible bird is able to reach speeds of up to 55 miles per hour and can fly continuously for days or even months. The wandering albatross relies on the high- and low-pressure air currents over the ocean to lift and carry it for these huge distances.

During the icy winter, the albatross is one of the few seabirds that does not fly north. Every few days the adult must return to feed its chick, left huddled in a nest on the edge of an island cliff. Although it can be almost covered by the falling snow, the chick is protected by thick down and a layer of insulating fat, while its parent spends the dark days over the cold Southern Ocean, searching diligently for food.

Figure 36 (right) Although this giant petrel chick looks harmless, once it is fully grown its powerful beak will cut through the thickest fur seal skin.

Among the Antarctic seabirds are garbage collectors, vultures, and pirates. Sheathbills, the only species without webbed feet, will eat almost anything—insects, seal excrement, dead animals, plants, and possibly their own eggs and chicks. Quick to spy any garbage, the sheathbills also dart between the legs of other feeding birds to snatch up any scraps. What they cannot eat will sometimes be used to build a nest—a messy collection of old bones, feathers, and scraps of fur from dead animals.

The vulture of the Antarctic seabirds is the giant petrel, often called the "glutton" or "stinkpot" by early whalers. These powerful birds not only feed on krill, they also steal chicks from penguin nurseries, and have been known to eat seaweed, seal guts, and even rope.

The pirates of the Antarctic, the skuas, are birds known for their daring. While fish, squid, and krill form their main food supply, they may also chase other birds, forcing them to cough up food to get an easy meal.

These birds supplement this diet with stolen penguin eggs and chicks. Stalking through a penguin colony, a skua will suddenly stab its hooked beak under a penguin, snatching out the egg. Sometimes they work in pairs, one bird grabbing the penguin while the other takes the egg.

Figure 38 (below) Although the skua lays two eggs, it only rears the first chick to hatch.

(Photo courtesy of Simon Ward)

Figure 37 Because it is difficult for the parents to find food, only half of the gray-headed albatross chicks survive.

(Photo courtesy of Kath Handasyde)

Early sightings

The idea of Terra Australis Incognita, the unknown land, has fascinated people for thousands of years.

As early as 400 B.C., a Greek philosopher called Parmenides claimed that the Earth was divided into five zones, including frozen regions at the two poles. Later philosophers put forward the idea of a great southern continent. In 729 A.D. in England, the Venerable Bede (an English monk) described the poles as eternally cold, with an ocean in the northern region and a vast land in the south.

In the 1300s and the 1400s in Europe, many believed the southern land to be one massive fertile continent stretching down to the South Pole. Although explorers searched the seas for this land mass, they were disappointed, discovering Australia, Kerguelen, South Georgia, South Shetland Island, and the Falkland Islands, but not the massive continent they expected.

The myth of the rich unknown land was finally shattered by British explorer Captain James Cook. In 1772 Cook put to sea in the *Resolution*, aiming to lead "discoveries as near to the South Pole as possible." In January 1773, he crossed the Antarctic Circle (66°32'S) and sailed the *Resolution* into "an immense field composed of different kinds of ice."

(Photo courtesy of Peter C. Gill)

The Antarctic continent was probably first seen by a Russian explorer, Thaddeus von Bellingshausen, on January 27, 1820. It is unlikely Bellingshausen recognized his view to be land: he described the sight as an "icefield" covered with small hills. In the same month, British Royal Navy Commander Edward Bransfield saw the Antarctic Peninsula.

For a year the ship attempted to move farther south, but it was stopped at 71°10'S by a huge ice wall. By February 1775 Cook had circumnavigated the continent without catching sight of land. Cook believed there was land

Figure 40 (right) In the 1300s and 1400s in Europe, some people believed that the undiscovered southern land would be a huge grassy continent with good soil for growing crops. As captured here by the early Antarctic photographer Frank Hurley, the southern land actually proved to be a land of ice and snow.

Figure 39 (below) Captain Cook could reach no farther into the Antarctic region than 71°10'S. Although unable to sight land, Cook prepared the way for future expeditions that eventually led to the discovery of Mt. Erebus, seen here across the Ross Sea.

(Photo courtesy of Museum of Victoria, Australia)

(Photo courtesy of Museum of Victoria, Australia)

Figure 41 This Antarctic-bound ship was named the *Aurora* after the famous "Southern Lights." The view is probably similar to the "immense field composed of different kinds of ice" seen by Captain James Cook.

in the region, but he considered it to be remote, desolate, and of no benefit to anyone.

Cook's report of large numbers of seals in these regions encouraged northern seal hunters to turn south in search of new hunting grounds. The charts of the sub-Antarctic islands produced on the *Resolution's* journey helped the sealers in their quest. Unfortunately, thousands of seals were killed for their fur, which was often used only for making slippers. By 1790, the "wealth" of the hunting ground led to the establishment of a sealing industry on the island of South Georgia. During the late 1700s, many more Antarctic and sub-Antarctic islands were discovered as the sealers extended their work into new areas.

In 1909, polar geographer Hugh R. Hill said, "... the desire to wipe out terra incognita appeals more deeply to certain instincts of human nature than either science or trade."

Feet on icy land

National expeditions in 1840 and 1841 advanced Antarctic exploration considerably. In 1840, while representing French interests, Dumont d'Urville laid claim to Terre Adelie, a stretch of Antarctica he named after his wife. Charles Wilkes, an American naval officer in charge of the United States Exploring Expedition, caught sight of the coastal region now called Wilkes Land.

In January 1841, an exploration led by British naval officer James Clark Ross was blocked by a huge ice shelf towering 150 to 240 feet above them and extending a further 820 feet below sea level. Ross wrote that in his attempt to sail farther south he "might with equal chance of success try to sail through the cliffs of Dover." It became known as the Ross Ice Shelf. Ross's other discoveries included Victoria Land, Mount Erebus, and Ross Island.

The only national expedition to enter the Southern Ocean during the next 55 years was the British HMS *Challenger* on its four-year scientific cruise. Although in 1895 the International Geographical Congress declared Antarctica the prime area for exploration, all claims for the first landing on the continent were made by sealers and whalers.

British sealer Andrew McFarlane and American sealer John Davis separately recorded landings, although the accuracy of their logs is still questioned.

Among those who could provide confirmed reports of their landing were whalers Henry Bull and Carsten Borchgrevinic. While it is agreed the landing occurred in 1895, exactly which man qualified as the first to step onto the Antarctic is still disputed.

In 1899, Carsten Borchgrevinic returned to the Antarctic on an expedition funded by a rich British publisher. The men with him

(Photo courtesy of the Australian Bureau of Meteorology)

Figures 42 a & b The Antarctic tent used by explorers, scientists, and researchers has developed over decades from an igloo-like hut (below) to models such as the modern red "apple" (right).

(Photo courtesy of Museum of Victoria, Australia)

aboard the *Southern Cross* were the first to spend a winter on the continent. Of that expedition, physicist Louis Bernacchi wrote, "The silence roared in our ears, it was centuries of heaped up solitude." The great icy continent, closed to humans for centuries, had finally recorded a small imprint, heralding the coming eras of exploration.

A Swede, Otto Nordenskjold, led one of the earliest voyages of the heroic age of Antarctic exploration. Arriving at the Antarctic Peninsula in February 1902, the *Antarctic* unloaded one group and returned later to collect them but was unable to reach the camp due to ice. A second group disembarked to lead the first to a meeting point. However, just beyond the peninsula the ship sank with those on board struggling to reach land. The three stranded groups, separated and without necessary supplies, miraculously survived the Antarctic winter and were rescued in the summer by an Argentinian ship.

Heroic explorers

The race to the Pole

Arriving in December 1911, the first party to reach the South Pole was headed by Norwegian, Roald Amundsen. Originally determined to be first to the North Pole, Amundsen and his sponsors changed their plans when Robert Peary arrived there first. Aware of the haste needed to achieve the mission, Amundsen's party used 52 dogs to pull their four sledges across the icecap. Traveling so quickly meant that the journey took them less time and they were able to carry less food, reducing the weight of their load.

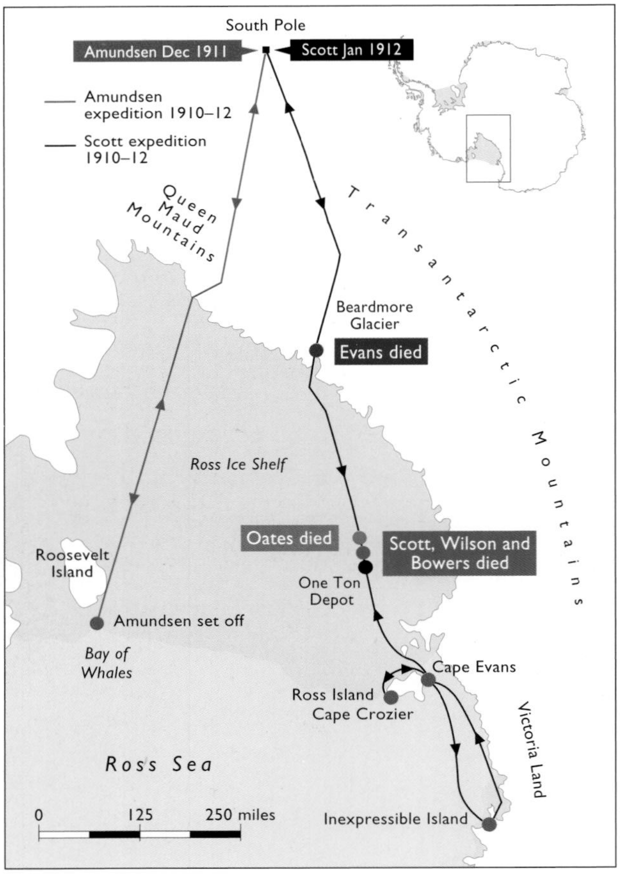

One of the most famous of the explorers of the heroic age was Britain's Robert Scott. Although his first attempt to reach the South Pole was forced to a halt by scurvy and snow blindness, Scott did reach his goal, arriving at the Pole on January 17, 1912. However, after traveling 1290 miles, pulling sleds carrying over 200 pounds each, the party learned that Amundsen had arrived four weeks before them. Scott was understandably disappointed: "Great God! This is an awful place and terrible enough for us to have labored to it without the reward of priority."

Figure 43 The routes taken by Amundsen and Scott.

Figure 44 Although Robert Scott's attempt to reach the South Pole ended tragically, his contribution to our knowledge of Antarctica is still recognized. Here he is seen writing in his journal.

(Photo courtesy of National Library of Australia)

Depression added to the problems of food shortage, frostbite, and scurvy. Petty Officer Evans died on February 17, while Captain Laurence Oates walked out into a blizzard, his feet gangrenous from frostbite. Scott and the two remaining members of his party died less than 14 days later, only 11 miles from a food depot which could have saved them.

Scott's motivation had not simply been to reach the South Pole and return. Sponsored by the Royal Geographical Society, Scott's expedition focused on scientific research. When the bodies of the three men were discovered the next spring, a sledge was found next to their tent, loaded with 35 pounds of fossil ferns embedded in rock. Without dogs to pull their sleds, Scott's party had dragged these specimens with them. In spite of their own fatigue, the men had refused to leave behind anything that might have been valuable to science.

Endurance

Another heroic British explorer was Ernest Shackleton, whose most noted expedition was an attempt to cross the Antarctic continent in 1914. His ship, the *Endurance*, became surrounded by ice in the Weddell Sea. Trapped aboard for the winter, the whole party had to abandon ship when the force of the pack ice crushed and sank the huge vessel. For the next five months the party drifted in their lifeboats, surviving on a diet of seal meat.

Eventually they made their way to Elephant Island where most stayed for four months, sheltering beneath their overturned boats. Six others, including Shackleton, traveled 800 miles to the western coast of South Georgia. They crossed a mountain range previously considered impossible to climb, and startled whalers at the Stromness station in May 1916. Those still stranded on Elephant Island were rescued shortly after.

Frank Hurley, the photographer aboard Ernest Shackleton's ill-fated 1914–16 expedition, was forced to abandon hundreds of photographic plates. Limited to only 120 plates, Hurley smashed the remaining images to stop himself from changing his mind.

As they were intended to pay for a large part of the expedition, the plates were given priority on the return voyage. At one point, valuable stores of food were thrown off the ship to make sure the 120 surviving photos reached their destination.

(Photo courtesy of National Library of Australia)

Figure 45 (above) This surviving photograph by Frank Hurley shows the dogs being unloaded from the ice-locked ship.

(Photo courtesy of Museum of Victoria, Australia)

Figure 46 Heroism was often expected of Antarctic explorers such as this group photographed by Frank Hurley. A newspaper advertisement placed by Ernest Shackleton read: "Men wanted for hazardous journey. Small wages, bitter cold, long months of complete darkness, constant danger, safe return doubtful. Honor and recognition in case of success."

Mawson: a case study in survival

A heroic act can be defined as a noble and courageous effort requiring determination, endurance, and extraordinary effort. One of the many Antarctic explorers who demonstrated these qualities was Australian geologist and explorer, Douglas Mawson.

Born in Yorkshire, England, in 1882, Mawson arrived in Australia when he was only two years old. At the age of 26, Mawson joined Shackleton's 1907–09 expedition. During the expedition Mawson, together with Australian, Tannatt W. Edgeworth David, and British naval surgeon, Alistair Mackay, arrived at the South Magnetic Pole—the first group ever to reach this point. The men trekked 1260 miles, pulling their sleds behind them. Edgeworth David later wrote that Mawson was "the soul of the march," praising his "splendid spirit, marvellous physique, and an indifference to frost and cold that was astonishing."

(Photo courtesy of Museum of Victoria, Australia)

Figure 47 Mawson (right), Mackay and Edgeworth David (center) plant the flag at the South Magnetic Pole on January 15, 1909.

Australian Antarctic Expedition

Douglas Mawson organized and led the first Australian expedition to Antarctica, which left Hobart in December 1911. In the summer of 1912–13, Mawson led an expedition to explore the far-eastern region around Commonwealth Bay; four other groups set out to cover the western, southern, and eastern regions. The group leaving Cape Denison on November 9, 1912 was Mawson, Lieutenant Belgrave Ninnis, and a Swiss doctor, Xavier Mertz. Aiming to reach the area previously trekked by Mawson, Mackay, and Edgeworth David, the men took along 16 husky dogs to speed the trip.

Tragedy

Disaster struck on December 14 when Ninnis was lost down a vast snow-covered crevasse. The treacherous glacial crack also swallowed the expedition's strongest dogs, the tent, extra clothing, and most of the food supplies. Forced to return, the two surviving men made them-

(Photo courtesy of Peter C. Gill)

Figure 48 Built in March 1912, Mawson's Hut at Cape Denison is being worn away by Antarctic ice and winds. Attempts have been made to preserve the building; some people have suggested that it be moved to Australia where it could be set up as a carefully maintained museum.

selves a makeshift tent using a tent cover and broken sledge runners, and set out on the 310-mile journey. Once their food supply was gone the men were forced to eat their dogs. On January 8 Mertz died, 100 miles from Cape Denison. It is likely that he died from toxic poisoning caused from eating the dogs' livers.

Mawson pushed on although he admitted he was "now so weak and starved there seemed little chance of my getting back, for there was a broad crevassed glacier ahead and highlands beyond to climb." At times he fell into such crevasses, saved only by his sledge which stayed on top. Each fall required an agonizing effort to climb out. With the soles of his feet bandaged, Mawson was sometimes forced to crawl on the ice, unable to walk due to the terrible pain.

When Mawson struggled to the base at Cape Denison on February 8, 1913, he could not be recognized. The first to reach him, Frank Bickerton, had to ask "Which one are you?" Missing most of his hair and skin, and with open splits on his face, Mawson had finally made it. Forced to spend another winter at the base, he was reported to have followed other members around during the first few weeks, needing to be near people after weeks of incredibly harsh loneliness. But Mawson had survived.

Technology on ice

Figure 49 Historically, technology has played an important part in Antarctic exploration. Seen here is the motor party from Scott's 1910–12 expedition.

(Photo courtesy of Popperfoto/Sporting Pix)

It was the great British explorer Robert Scott who first ascended into the Antarctic skies. On February 4, 1902, Scott went up 490 feet in a hot air balloon called *Eva*. Of that feat he wrote: "The honor of being the first aeronaut in Antarctica ... I chose for myself." However, once in the chilled air, Scott had second thoughts: "As I swayed in what appeared to be a very inadequate basket and gazed down on the rapidly diminishing figures below, I felt some doubt as to whether I had been wise in my choice."

Others who saw the Antarctic ice from a balloon included Ernest Shackleton who, along with Scott, is noted as the first aerial photographer of the Antarctic continent.

German Erich von Drygalski also went up, but to twice the height of the other men. In the air, von Drygalski commented, "It's so warm up here I can even take off my gloves." Although others also reached the sky via hot air balloons, their view of the continent was still very limited.

Among those who recognized the benefits of technology in the Antarctic was Douglas Mawson, who brought over a wireless telegraph for radio communication. It is claimed that Mawson also aimed to be the first

Figure 50 With the development of radio echo-sounding carried out from aircraft, the thickness and layering of the ice can be measured more accurately. Lakes and mountain ranges have been discovered using this method.

(Photo courtesy of Museum of Victoria, Australia)

to use aircraft in Antarctica, but the plane he had hoped to use was damaged during a practice flight in Adelaide.

It was Hubert Wilkins who, on November 16, 1928, made the first airplane flight in Antarctica. Wilkins had been a member of Shackleton's 1922 expedition aboard the *Quest* and was able to compare the struggle of land exploration with the new dimension added by air travel: "It had taken us three months on foot to map 40 miles: now we were covering 40 miles in 20 minutes ... I was thrilled to realize that ... for the first time in human history, new land was being discovered from the air."

The honor of being the first to fly to the South Pole is held by Americans Richard Byrd and Bernt Balchen: they reached the pole in November 1929. Although aircraft had opened up territories previously unseen, their technology was not error-free. Wilkins and another explorer, Lincoln Ellsworth, thought

(Photo courtesy of Honda)

Figure 51 The Honda TRX 300 FW all-terrain cycle has helped to speed up travel on the ice.

they had found "Stefansson Strait," a body of ice-covered water that cut through the Antarctic Peninsula. In fact, no such strait exists.

One of Robert Scott's 1912 party, Dr. Edward Wilson, declared: "When polar exploration becomes possible to a flying machine, its attraction to most people will be finished." Continued scientific flights and the introduction of Antarctic air tourism have proven Wilson's prophecy wrong. However, caution is needed to make sure the precious wilderness is not damaged by any undue interference from technology.

The ozone "hole"

Different ideas have been circulated about the Antarctic ozone "hole"; its size, origin, and effect on human beings have been discussed in scientific communities and the media around the world. The "hole" is actually a thinning of the layer of ozone that exists in the stratosphere, 6 to 30 miles above the Earth.

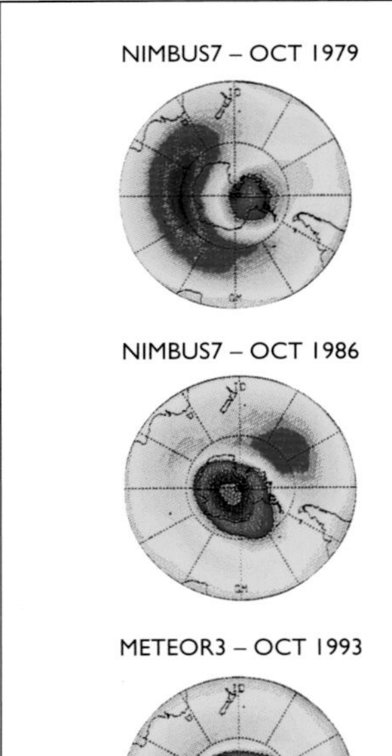

Figure 52 Data gathered between 1979 and 1993 show the change in the size and shape of the Antarctic ozone "hole" over a period of almost 15 years.

(Imagery courtesy of Ozone Unit, Australian Bureau of Meteorology)

Ozone, a poisonous molecule of three oxygen atoms (O_3), is formed when ultraviolet radiation from the sun is absorbed by the two-atom oxygen (O_2). Although ozone forms only one part in three million in the Earth's atmosphere, it is important because it protects the Earth from harmful ultraviolet (UV) radiation.

Ozone levels have been measured and recorded since the 1950s, but it wasn't until 1981 that a British scientist observed the springtime "hole" over Antarctica. The thinning has continued, and in the spring of 1993 the amount of ozone in the atmosphere was half that recorded in the 1950s.

The natural rate at which ozone is broken down has been increased by high levels of chlorofluorocarbons (CFCs). CFCs are chemicals that are commonly used in refrigerators, air conditioners, foam plastics, and pressurized sprays. In Antarctica, the winter winds and extreme cold trap CFCs in ice crystal clouds. The CFCs react with sunlight in the early spring, producing ozone-destroying chlorine atoms. As a result of this process a "hole" appears in September, recovering to normal levels by late spring or early summer.

Without sufficient ozone, a greater percentage of ultraviolet rays reach the Earth. UV rays are known to cause skin cancer, eye cataracts, genetic damage, and a weakening of disease-fighting systems in humans, as well as problems with some plant crops. In the Antarctic, the food chain may be threatened as the continued depletion of ozone may reduce populations of krill and phytoplankton, which are important in the diet of many types of birds, whales, penguins, and seals.

International concern about ozone depletion has led to action. In 1987, the United Nations Environment Program introduced a "Protocol on Substances that Deplete the Ozone Layer," which introduced measures to limit CFC production. Substitute products are now being

(Image courtesy of NASA Goddard Space Flight Center)

(Photo courtesy of the Australian Bureau of Meteorology)

Figure 53 (left) Produced from data gathered on October 6, 1987, this three-dimensional image represents the ozone "hole" in highs and lows. The darker colors represent the areas where there is a lower concentration of ozone.

Figure 54 (below) Exactly how the ozone "hole" might affect the Antarctic continent and its wildlife is a subject that scientists continue to study.

introduced—many household sprays now carry "ozone friendly" and "No CFCs" labels.

Concerns are also being raised about another chemical, methyl bromide, which is also known to destroy ozone. Methyl bromide is sometimes used for soil fumigation and occurs in exhaust fumes from vehicles burning leaded petrol and in large-scale burning of vegetation. It is also produced naturally by the ocean. Recommendations are being made to reduce the amount of methyl bromide produced.

Although most CFCs are released in the northern hemisphere, there is no corresponding ozone "hole" over the Arctic region. This is because the Antarctic features a land mass surrounded by ocean, creating low temperatures in the stratosphere. In these low temperatures, clouds form—clouds in which the chemical changes leading to ozone destruction occur. The Arctic has no land mass, so the air in the stratosphere is warmer. The clouds typical of the Antarctic do not form there, so ozone depletion in the Arctic is occurring more slowly.

Environmental concerns

In 1991, an Environmental Protocol was signed with the aim of keeping Antarctica "a natural reserve, devoted to peace and science." Since the earliest explorers, the human presence in Antarctica has challenged these aims, at times disrupting the environment and giving science free reign, regardless of the cost to nature.

Although the consequence of these acts may be unintentional, the damage can be permanent. Organizations such as the Scientific Committee for Antarctic Research (SCAR) and Greenpeace continue to draw attention to environmental concerns.

Impact of the bases

Eager to learn from the vast wilderness, those involved in establishing research bases were not always aware of the potential problems they were creating. SCAR reported that research stations were often built "for either logistical [practical] or scientific reasons and without thought for environmental effects."

For example, four bases have been built on the Fildes Peninsula, a special area previously set aside because of the rich plant and animal life it supported. Unfortunately, this situation has gone from bad to worse, with road construction damaging even more of the area's moss growth.

Waste disposal is also a problem. Many bases choose to incinerate waste material such as paper products and food scraps. The unfiltered

(Photo courtesy of Greg Mortimer)

Figure 56 (above) Waste dumped from Antarctic bases not only spoils the beautiful landscape, but can also threaten wildlife which scavenge amongst the rubbish.

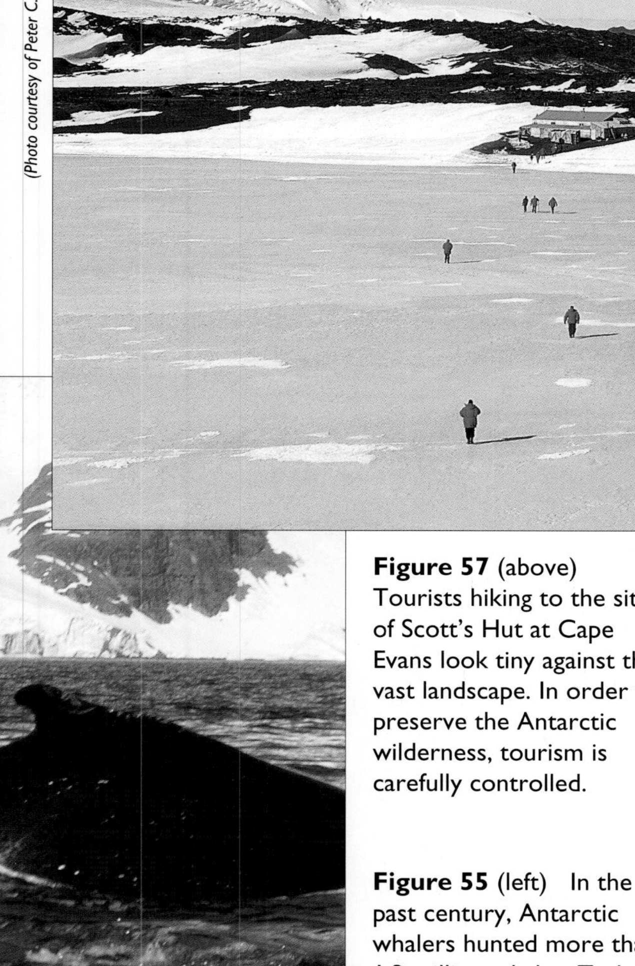

(Photo courtesy of Peter C. Gill)

Figure 57 (above) Tourists hiking to the site of Scott's Hut at Cape Evans look tiny against the vast landscape. In order to preserve the Antarctic wilderness, tourism is carefully controlled.

Figure 55 (left) In the past century, Antarctic whalers hunted more than 1.3 million whales. Today, tourists visiting Antarctica are instructed not to disturb or harm any of the region's wildlife.

Figure 58 A red "apple" tent glows beneath an Antarctic moon. When used with care, these temporary shelters leave little evidence of human presence.

(Photo courtesy of the Australian Bureau of Meteorology)

A devastating airstrip

At Dumont d'Urville a base was built to study the unusual wealth of flora and fauna in the region, including an emperor penguin colony. Although this site looked like a scientific treasure-chest, the base is ice-locked for 10 months of the year. The French government talked about solving this problem, but made no formal proposals.

Unannounced, work began in January 1983 on the construction of an airstrip on the chain of islands close to the base—the Pointe Geologie Archipelago.

Dynamite blasting leveled the earth to build the hard-rock runway, but it also destroyed the homes of 8000 birds. Penguins and seabirds were killed by the blasting and the breeding grounds of eight species of seabirds were ruined.

In January 1994, an unusually large wave caused by ice falling from the Astrolabe glacier damaged the hangar and runway. Since then the airstrip has not been repaired for landings.

smoke may carry toxic cancer-forming chemicals, ash, and metal particles that pollute Antarctica's air and water.

Stations pumping sewage into the sea also damage the region. Human sewage contains bacteria and high levels of nitrates and phosphates that could pollute the ocean and disrupt its natural balance.

Even food scraps can cause trouble. Although the protocol bans feeding wildlife, some stations are careless and the predatory skuas feed off their garbage. One station was known to host 200 skuas, an artificially large population that could upset the local food chain.

Poor waste management, toxic leaks, fuel spills, overfishing, and global pollution all threaten the land and wildlife of Antarctica. The success of solutions relies on people caring enough about the state of the continent to obey regulations. All nations must be willing to protect the part of the ice they are privileged to use.

MODERN ISSUES IN AN OLD WORLD

Toward a world park

No one and everyone owns Antarctica. When the initial age of exploration had passed there was confusion and competition over ownership of different parts of the continent. In 1950, in celebration of the Third Polar Year, Antarctica was chosen as one of two regions of study. Scientists from 67 countries worked together—initially for 18 months—and the project's success led to the establishment of the Scientific Committee for Antarctic Research.

With this basis for international cooperation, the Antarctic Treaty was signed in 1959. Its purpose is to protect the continent. Of the twelve nations that initially joined, seven had previously claimed territory. To reduce any disputes over ownership, the Treaty specifically avoids recognizing such claims.

The activity on the 37 permanent research stations provides valuable information about the vast network of life on the continent. Those who work and live in the stations face extreme conditions. About 800 winter residents face long periods of darkness and social isolation, and have little physical contact with the world outside. Their experience is so similar to that of space travelers that research is now being conducted on Antarctic residents to better understand the stresses faced by astronauts.

Antarctica offers much to the rest of the world: as a spectacular and rugged wilderness, as a field for research, and as a record of the past. To preserve the wilderness, proposals have been made to establish Antarctica as a world park with careful restrictions on the number of visitors. International cooperation, environmentally friendly research, careful small-scale tourism, and appropriate protection of plants and animals would be features of the park. It is hoped that by the year 2000 this vision of Antarctica will be a reality.

(Photo courtesy of Peter C. Gill)

Figure 59 World Park Antarctica is the goal of many individuals and groups determined to preserve one of the world's last wilderness areas.

Glossary

Antarctic Convergence (Also known as the Antarctic Polar Front.) The band of water around Antarctica where cold currents from the south meet warmer currents from the north.

asteroids Lumps of rock and ice that orbit the sun between Mars and Jupiter.

aurora australis (Also known as the Southern Lights.) A spectacular display of colored light in the night sky, caused by magnetic particles from the sun.

baleen plates Plates fringed with bristles that some whales have instead of teeth. They use them to strain sea water to extract food such as krill.

bedrock The solid rock beneath the thick layer of ice that covers Antarctica.

blizzard A severe snowstorm with very strong winds.

calving The process in which icebergs break away from ice shelves and glaciers on the edge of the Antarctic continent.

CFCs Chlorofluorocarbons: one of the main groups of chemicals responsible for ozone reduction.

circumnavigate To sail completely around something (usually a continent or the whole world).

circumpolar current A strong ocean current that flows from the Antarctic region in a northwesterly direction.

crevasse A deep crack in the ice.

cyclone A violent, destructive wind storm.

dog sun (Also known as "mock sun.") A ring of light that forms around the sun due to ice crystals in the air.

ecosystem The interconnected web of plant and animal life that survives in a particular environment.

fast ice The thick, solid ice that permanently covers the land mass of Antarctica.

food chain The sequence of plants and animals that eat and are eaten by one another.

glacier A mass of ice that moves very slowly across the land.

Gondwana A "supercontinent" that probably existed up until 160 million years ago. It consisted of what are now Australia, Africa, South America, India, and New Zealand.

halo A ring of light that forms around the sun or moon due to ice crystals in the air.

harem A group of female animals guarded over by a single male.

hemoglobin A red substance in the blood that carries oxygen.

ice core A long tube of ice obtained by drilling into the icecap.

icebow A display of colored light, like a rainbow, that appears on the ice.

icecap The permanent covering of ice at the North and South Poles.

incubation Keeping eggs warm (usually by sitting on them) until they hatch.

katabatic winds Downward-flowing winds often occurring in central Antarctica.

lunar Of or from the moon.

marine Of or from the sea.

meteorite A rock from outer space that falls to Earth.

meteorologist A scientist who studies the weather.

molting The process in which birds lose one set of feathers and replace them with a new set.

NASA National Aeronautics and Space Administration (of the U.S.A.).

ozone "hole" The thinning of the ozone layer that occurs over Antarctica every southern spring.

pack ice Floating sheets of ice.

photosynthesis The process in which plants convert sunlight into nutrients (food).

SCAR Scientific Committee for Antarctic Research.

South Magnetic Pole The southern pole of the Earth's magnetic field. Compass needles point to the magnetic North and South Poles. The South Magnetic Pole is about 170 miles from the South Pole.

South Pole The southernmost point of the Earth.

spawn Fish eggs. (Also the process of producing them.)

species A group of plants or animals that have some common features and can breed with one another.

sub-Antarctic Areas immediately to the north of the Antarctic Polar Front.

sun pillar A column of light that is caused by ice crystals in the air.

supercontinent A huge land mass that existed hundreds of millions of years ago and which broke up to form what are now separate continents.

Terra Australis Incognita The "unknown southern land" which was believed to exist by European philosophers from as early as 400 B.C.

whiteout A condition that occurs in Antarctica when the sky is covered with even white cloud so that no shadows fall on the ice, making it difficult to judge distances and angles.

wilderness An area of land that exists in its natural state.

Index

aircraft 40–41
algae 16–17
all-terrain cycles 41
Amundsen, Roald 36, 37
Antarctic Circle 6, 11, 32
Antarctic Convergence 6
Antarctic Peninsula 6, 9, 17, 33, 35
Antarctic Treaty 46
aurora australis 14
Balchen, Bernt 41
Bellingshausen, Thaddeus von 33
Bernacchi, Louis 34
birds 18, 19, 42, 44–45
  see also penguins, seabirds
Borchgrevenic, Carsten 34
Bransfield, Edward 33
Bull, Henry 34
Byrd, Richard 41
Cape Denison 38
CFCs 42–43
circumpolar current 9
climate *see* weather
Commonwealth Bay 6, 38
conservation 43, 44–46
Cook, James 4, 32
Crossley, Louise 15
cyclones 8
d'Urville, Dumont 34
Davis, John 34
dinosaurs 4
dogs 36, 37, 38, 39
Dry Valleys 4, 6, 12, 13, 16
Drygalski, Erich von 40
Edgeworth David, Tannatt 38
Elephant Island 37
environmental issues 42–46
explorers 32–41, 44
fish 18, 19, 28–29, 31
food chains 18–19, 31, 42
fungi 16–17
geology 6, 7
glaciers 6, 7, 9, 45
Gondwana 5
hot air balloons 40
Hurley, Frank 33
icebergs 8–9, 17
krill 18–19, 21, 27, 31, 42
lichen 16–17
Mackay, Alistair 38
Mawson (Australian research base) 6, 15
Mawson, Douglas 5, 13, 38–41
McFarlane, Andrew 34
Mertz, Xavier 38, 39
meteorites 13
moss 16–17, 44
Mount Erebus 6, 32, 34
NASA 4, 12
Ninnis, Belgrave 38
Nordenskjold, Otto 35
ozone "hole" 42–43
penguins 5, 19, 22–25, 27, 31, 42, 45
phytoplankton 18–19, 42
plants 16–19, 44
research bases 6, 44–46
Ross Ice Shelf 6, 9, 34
Ross Island 6, 34
Ross, James Clark 34
science 4, 11, 12–13, 40–46
Scott, Robert 36, 37, 40, 41
seabirds 19, 22–23, 30–31, 44–45
  see also birds, penguins
sealers 27, 32–33, 34
seals 18, 19, 20, 23, 26–27, 31, 32–33, 42
Shackleton, Ernest 37, 38, 40, 41
South Georgia 33, 37
South Magnetic Pole 6, 38
South Pole 6, 11, 32, 36, 37, 41
Southern Ocean 6, 7, 8–9, 18, 20, 26, 28, 30, 34
squid 18, 19, 31
temperature 5, 10, 16, 28, 43
tents 34, 35, 44
tourism 45
Trans-Antarctic Mountains 6, 7
Victoria Land 6, 34
weather 5, 8, 10–11, 14–15, 16
Weddell Sea 7, 37
whalers 20, 34, 45
whales 18, 19, 20–21, 23, 42, 45
whiteout 14
Wilkes Land 7, 34
Wilkes, Charles 34
Wilkins, Hubert 41
Wilson, Edward 41